CW00555010

# IN BET
# GO AND STOP

## COLLECTED POEMS

## Ruth Parker

© Ruth Parker 2006

Poetry Monthly Press

## Acknowledgements:

This book is dedicated with love to my husband Reg and to all my family and friends who have been the inspiration of much of my work.
Thanks are also due to Martin Holroyd, my hardworking editor, to Simon Fletcher for his good advice and to Albrighton Writers' Circle whose encouragement has always given me that extra 'push' to put something on paper.

These poems have appeared in several anthologies and in many magazines, including:
*Dial 174, Eclipse, Enrichment in Verse, Helicon, Iota, Warwick University's 'the magazine', West Midlands Arts 'People to People', Poetry Digest, Poetry Monthly, Reach, Salopeot, Select Magazine, and Quantum Leap.*

# CONTENTS

## Amadepus

Yes, I think Mozart would have liked cats —
Their intricate weaving,
Their rhythmical heaving
Would have found an echo in the master's heart.

Would he have liked to hear cats?
Their "Nightmusic" is cruder,
But he too often was ruder
Than one would have guessed for a man of such infinite art.

I do think Mozart would have taken to cats —
Their rhapsodic rumblings
And operatic grumblings
Must have raised a smile on his part.

But I fear that Mozart had no chance to like cats —
With his feverish working,
(Poverty always lurking),
And being so young when he had to depart —
I ***wish*** Mozart could have enjoyed cats.

## Haiku

Necklace of Haiku
Seventeen syllables, each
One a gleaming pearl.

## Friends

Friends
are like the flesh on your bones.
Without them
each blow, each knock,
each juddering shock
would strike straight to the marrow.
With them, we are
lightly anaesthetised,
slightly immunised
against various ills,
troubles and spills
programmed for us in life's circus.

So, how do they do it?
They listen...

## Haiku

Snow says it's winter —
Only your warmth puts back the
Spring in my step.

## The Odd Couple

"We do the daftest things," they said,
Smiling at me, together on the sofa,
"We wake at odd times in the night
And make ourselves a cup of tea;
Then we may chat and talk for hours
Until we see the sun come up,
And then we go to sleep!"

Not daft, but happy," I replied,
And joined in, laughing with them,
Not knowing that in a few weeks time
The younger and stronger of the two
Would be no more.

So, poor old man,
Whom do you chat to now
When the sun rises and
You see the aching gap
Beside you in the bed?

## Haiku

Autumn leaves dropping,
Warm golden colours, not grey
Like my falling hair

## Armchair Traveller

The old woman, tied to her chair by pain
Gazes out at the Midland rain,
But in her mind's eye, she can see the crest,
The mighty towers of Everest.

She sits and stirs in her hard wooden chair
Smelling the damp and fume-filled air,
But in her ears are the splash and the dip
Of porpoises larking as they follow her ship.

She sits and waits to be put to bed
But the pictures continue the show in her head.
And as she snugs the shawl round her arms
She can feel the swaying of coconut palms.

She stretches her limbs and flexes her back,
Peers at the wallpaper's splintering crack,
But inwardly, as the one bar glows
She is viewing the splendours of eternal snows.

## Haiku

Soft rain gleams like pearls;
How I wish I could wear them
Instead of my tears.

## Widows

*(After watching Alan Whicker)*

They wear their carapace of gutsiness and humour,
Shining examples of reliability,
But inwardly they're haunted by the aching thought
Whom can I lean on - who will comfort ME?

They sport their shells of imperturbability,
Willing to help, support their friends,
But in the silence of their tidy homes they cry,
Whom can I tell it to when this day ends?

They show their outer skins of cheerfulness,
Travelling fast - frantic to fly,
But waking early in a foreign room they ask
Where am I going to - and why?

## Bosnia

Whatever the battle
Whatever the war
Whatever they've all been fighting for
If it's defence or if it's attack
At the end, we see the old women in black
Wringing their hands and weeping.

## Grow Old Along With Us

We're growing old together now
my cat and I,
only she's ageing at a faster rate,
having already overreached
a century,
whereas my score is a mere
sixty up to date.
She is half deaf and
nearly blind
but I can hear and with the
aid of specs
can see quite well. We still possess
our sense of smell
and so I know that she
no longer has
that freshly windblown scent of a
fit outdoor cat —
it seems she's now a little careless
with her toiletry,
(thank God I'm still in control
of mine).
The two of us have aching joints that make us
loath to stir,
but when we're stroked there is
no doubt
we've not forgotten how
to purr!

## Penny At Nearly 21
## or Preserving The Spark

The old cat looks at me
With troubled opaque eyes
And pleads
Oh mother, wind me up,
I'm running down —
I feel the hard cold creeping
Fast along my spine,
My blood is chilled
My bones are aching,
Let your warmth stoke
My engine,
Let your touch fan
My embers
Before I'm down to ash,
Before I'm swallowed up
By the harsh darkness.

I pick her up,
Stroking her scrawny belly,
Fondling her downy ears,
And then the spark rekindles,
The engine purrs,
And she begins to glow,
Her body seems to grow
And the cold is kept at bay
At least for one more day.

## Women on Men

Blinkered, they plough on
regardless.
"One thing at a time," they
snap,
putting full weight behind their
concentration.
"Can you manage to ***breathe*** while you're working?"
we ask —
they're too absorbed to hear the implied
condemnation.

We lesser creatures, perform
simultaneously
cooking and counselling, animal
husbandry
and in between, while weeding the
garden
we think up a poem into the
bargain.

We need to be Jill of all trades but mistress
of ALL —
will no one admit this is rather a tall
order?

## Almost a Stable

What is bliss?
This is:
Baby on one arm,
cat on the other,
all breathing softly
We warm one another.
Child gurgles gently,
Slips into dozing,
Cat's tongue protrudes,
His eyes are closing;
Me in the middle,
A blessed Trinity —
Babe, woman, cat,
(But we claim no divinity)
Ignoring the future, forgetting the past,
The present is bliss - but how long will it last.?

## Succulent

The plant you gave me flourishes in
luxuriant splendour —
fat finger leaves, wide throated flowers,
unlike our friendship, which curled up
and died.

## Cat Woman of Wolverhampton

When I am well and truly old
I think I will become the local cat woman.
As soon as they hear me lift the latch,
When they catch the slurp of my slippers
the cats will come running
squeezing through hedges, sliding under fences,
bursting from cat flaps they will come,
flourishing tails in greeting,
butting their noses into my Nora Batty wrinkles
opening wide, triangular mouths,
doing their damnedest to look neglected.
I will place the bowls on the ground
and they will gorge themselves on my offerings,
heads down, tails now neatly packed away.
After that, a quiet moment of reflective grooming,
rough tongues will scrape at tainted fur,
distended bellies resonant with rumblings.
They will give me a cursory rub in acknowledgement,
submit to having stomachs tickled,
eyes slitted in intense enjoyment,
then suddenly they will be off
on some mysterious feline errands.

Having sat and watched them
and revelled in their satisfaction
I will go back inside, feeling
that for one half hour at least
I have been needed.

## A Dry Eye in the House

The doctor says
The liquid in your eyes
isn't up to scratch —
I will prescribe
***Artificial tears.***
The patient replies,
"That confirms my worst fears:
I find it extremely trying
That ***I*** now have to have help
With my crying!
It's an utter disgrace —"
And he laughed till he cried
And the tears failed to run down his face.

## No Uncle Remus

Last night I was woken by
the harsh, intrusive screeching
of a vixen,
brazen it was and lustful,
unafraid, sure that she was top dog
in our urban jungle.

This morning, on the lawn
the decapitated body
of a blackbird.
Good old Brer Fox and his Missus -
not so cosy...

## Once a refugee...

For years I've lived a calm and happy life
Blessed with affection and with beauty all around me,
But as a child I left a vicious land
And many loved ones who were not allowed
To end their lives serenely in their beds.
So, often when I look at my content
I ask myself, "What have I done —
Why have ***I*** been the lucky one?"

And every night, as sure as fate
I run for trains - but I'm too late;
Gasping, I rush for buses that leave as I arrive,
My car takes me to fearful unknown places as I drive;
I struggle against mud, slipping and sliding,
Faceless pursuers force me into hiding.
I cry for help by telephone,
The line is dead - I am alone...
All night I must continue striving,
Stumbling and straining, not arriving;
And when I wake, I have the strange and subtle dread
Had I arrived - I think I would be dead!

Still this is not too much to bear
In view of the great suffering everywhere —
It's only just a minor scar
Left over from another war,
And it's the price I have to pay
For being alive in my home today.

And then at night, as sure as fate
The train has left and I'm too late...

## Fame is the Spur

To be praised posthumously
Wouldn't amuse me
One little bit.
To be spoken of with pride
When I've crossed the Great Divide
Is no use to me.
To be lauded to the skies
When they come to close my eyes
Brings no joy to me
To be universally read
When I'm definitely dead
Sound no fun to me.
***SO***
Let's have a little fame today
Let me be able to make hay
While the sun shines,
While people read my lines,
And after that I'll go
No fuss, no affray
I'll go quietly. OK?
I'LL go
Because I'll know
I'll be remembered.

## ...Lingua Franca

*For Lucy*

The two year old, speaking childhood's language
Stands pointing urgently.
Stabbing the air,
Like a stranger in a foreign city,
Trying her best to be understood —
And failing...

## Mulberry at Dudmaston

'Oh look at that old tree',
they said,
'just like a shipwreck —
or a pile of driftwood washed up
on the beach.'
But stepping closer we could see
each brittle twig
each twisted branch
was swelling with new growth.
'Bet YOU would not be sprouting buds
after four hundred years.'
we said - and they agreed.

## Comfort

When I was small
I used to love the time
When I'd been put to bed
And heard my teacher aunt
Come in, sit herself down,
Ready to mark her books;
And in the mellow light of the half-covered lamp
I'd snooze,
Soothed by the gentle scratching of her pen
And the rustling of the pages.

Even now, very much older,
I find great happiness, my dear,
From hearing you in the next bed,
Clearing your throat, sighing softly,
Rustling the sheets,
And knowing, that unlike
So many of my friends,
I am not alone!

## None So Strange

It seems very odd
that while some parts of the world
are killing each other
because of their histories,
other parts are lying peacefully in bed
reading murder mysteries!

## Unreasonable Behaviour

I nearly set myself on fire last night
While toasting bread for tea,
And find the line is very slight
'Twixt farce and tragedy.
The scene was calm - Brahms on the air —
The toast was nicely turning,
I took it down without much care
And found my sleeve was burning!

I rushed to douse the scorching spot,
But soon, while it was soaking
Felt that my back was getting hot —
The dress itself was smoking!

I start to rip and tear it off,
Plunging it into water:
The grizzly tatters make me cough —
Remind me of bomb slaughter.

Unharmed, I find someone to blame,
Hear Brahms - serenely yearning,
"How dare you play while I'm aflame —
Fiddling while I am burning!"

## Haiku

Rosebuds of Summer
Herald dawns of delight for
Marauding greenfly.

## Dear Trazom

How can I
who can only fumble and plod
dare to praise you?
But it's only YOUR gifts
that could make me believe in a
bountiful God.

*Mozart liked to sign his name backwards,*
*as one of his jokes*

## The Moving Finger Writes...

The good thing about time is
that it doesn't stand still;
it may creep or crawl or seem to hover
but it IS always moving on,
even in the sickly hours of the night when
its digital face coldly blinks the slow
minutes away.
Just think how terrifying it would be
if time stayed for ever at ten past three,
forever still, in the dark, heartless hours of the night.

## Post Christmas

Christmas is over now
No need to dive for cover now
The battle has been won —
But at what cost?
What a cannonade of carols
What a militancy of mincepies
What a bombardment of baubles
What a fusillade of fir trees
What a skirmish of sweetmeats
What a parade of puddings
What an arsenal of alcohol
We have had to get through!

Now that peace reigns
We can cast off
Our uniforms of smiles
Our medals of good humour
And revert relievedly
To the bad-tempered mufti
Of our normal truculence.

We plan to sulk comfortably
Until next December.

## Haiku

Babe in the manger.
Time to light candles of joy...
Time to light fuses...

## Insomniac's Mantra

*(To be chanted three times after lights-out)*

I'm resting —
just testing my
tiredness.

I'm relaxing —
not taxing my
energies.

I'm dozing —
life's posing no
questions now.

I'm snoozing —
I'm losing my
anxieties.

I'm slumbering —
keep numbering those
jumping sheep.

I'm dreaming —
slowly steaming to
Nirvana Land.

Good night everyone,
I've been, come and gone,
I'm sinking down deep,
I'm falling asleep —
Good night!

## Appearances

*(Written for Alzheimer's Disease Week)*

They come in holding hands,
A well-dressed couple, middle aged;
It's good, I thought, that they still need to touch
In these their greyer and more sober years.
And then she dropped his hand for just one second —
At once I saw the terror in his eyes:
He was a child left on a desert island,
The sea of humans broiling round him,
And he not knowing who he was or what to do.

## Adult Education

"Oh when I hear that swoop
in Bruckner's Mass in E,
I feel I am transfigured
into another me —
out of myself I float and rise,"
she said, the sparks of fervour glinting
in her blue, eighty-five year old eyes.

# Lines Written in January ’95

*(Shows things don’t change much)*

Bosnia is erupting
Chechnya is aflame
Africa is starving
Everyone’s to blame.
The Antarctic is quietly melting
The ozone layer is rent
Pumas are prowling in Dorset
The N.H.S. budget is spent.
Calves are sent to Europe
Like sardines packed in tins
But beggars in our large cities
Are eating their meals out of bins
There’s radio-active material
Left on a rubbish dump
And cantankerous Tory rebels
Are giving the P.M. the hump;
But when I look at the heavens
A wonderful sight meets my eye
And my heart leaps up with Wordsworth’s
At the rainbow in the sky!

## Awakening

When I wake early before dawn
A cloud descends on me
Of petty worries, trivial doubts,
until I hear your gentle breathing;
you clear your throat, rustle the sheets
and then I know I'm not alone
and it is safe to go to sleep again.

## Touching Wood

When we two part, even if only for a day
We always 'Kiss each other safe':
Brow, chin, then on each cheek,
Up, down and side to side.
How strange it is that we,
Agnostic doubters that we are,
Should carry out this exact ritual
To ensure safe travelling and prompt arrival
With the age old symbol of the Cross!

## Surprise, Surprise!

While I was peeling carrots at the sink
Some radio music made me stop and think,
Who's written that, what can it be?
That music's getting through to me!
It isn't classical -  that's plain to hear,
It can't be modern, since I cannot bear
Those discords, that cacophony;
No, this stuff is entrancing me -
Poignant and tender - almost haunting,
Not those abrasive notes I find so daunting.
Then, as the strains came to their thrilling close,
My hands grew still, my fingers froze;
Composer Schonberg - fancy that,
Now I will have to go and eat my hat!

## Ebb Tide

When you put out
the light
a wave of darkness
cools my eyes
and nudges me
into the pool
of sleep.

## Festina Lente

*(or, More Hurry, Less Speed)*

Little Miss Muff was fixated on speed,
Hurtling about was her greatest need;
She scorched, she scudded, she streaked, she sped,
She charged like storm troopers heroically led.
But alas, one day, she caught her foot on a stair
And plunged to her fate with spectacular flair.
The funeral rites were succinct and brief
Giving her friends little chance for grief,
But later they trotted off to a wake,
In a Fast Food Cafe, for their dead pal's sake.

Meanwhile Miss Muff, no longer in haste
Lay gravely concerned - she'd got time to waste!

## Haiku

Old age is a curse.
We have one consolation
There IS something worse.

## The Kraken (Japanese Earthquake, 1995)

How thin this crust on which our world is based
With all our modern artifacts laid waste
When the great beast heaves just one turn,
Our roads collapse, our bridges burn.
Nature's still red in tooth and claw
Following its own chaotic law;
Even our trains, our 'phones, each vital fax
Slither into her steaming cracks —
Chasms appear, skyscrapers drop,
The underworld's come out on top
And nature's reclaiming her kingdom.

## Tsunami

When the big wave came
and devoured the innocents
did it also snatch
the predators, the killers?

Oh no -

crocodiles are flexing their jaws
vultures are circling...

## Pottery Siamese

*(Sonnet in memory of Penny)*

This is the very essence of our cat:
Her creamy flanks arranged in regal pose,
Brown tail curled round except for one inch that
Points sharply up; we see her shapely nose,
The triangles of ears milk-chocolate dipped.
But where's the warmth of body and of fur?
Where the soft lap of milk secretly sipped?
Where the response, where the resounding purr?
Her blue eyes stare with glassy, knowing gaze,
But where's the blink of those endearing eyes?
And when I stroke her form, my fingers graze,
My ring clangs harshly on her hollow thighs.
        This cat I cannot love, try as I may,
        Her heart is cold and she has feet of clay.

## Haiku

Smog - grubby grey cat
Crouches on my throat, its hairs
Blocking my breathing.

## Biloxi Blues

*(Hurricane Katrina)*

Civilization's crust is very thin,
It gleams and glows in multi-coloured lights.
But when you look beneath its polished skin
Nature is lurking to assert her rights.
Where is the music, where the ease and laughter
When waves break in and sweep your all away?
No food, no shelter and no drinking water,
With death around you, sickness and decay.
The weak go to the wall, the savage thrive,
Those who give aid are ruthless killers' prey,
The strongest, fiercest manage to survive,
Only brute force will keep their crimes at bay.
So when the world seems orderly and neat
Is the ground safe beneath our careless feet?

## Haiku

The New Year comes in
Like a rip-roaring lion —
The poor are its prey

## Sonnet For A Twentieth Century Blessing

What joy it is to own a microwave
Dealing with puddings, vegetables and meat,
The busy housewife's ever willing slave —
No need for labouring in fumes and heat;
The husband's friend when he is left alone,
Speedily serving him his pre-cooked meal,
Transforming a potato hard as stone
Into a fluffy treat, down to its peel.
Our early morning porridge is prepared
Whilst we still yawn, before our eyes can blink,
And through its magic workings we are spared
Hours of scrubbing saucepans at the sink.

In praises of the microwave I sing —
Long may we listen for its welcome ping-ping-ping-ping-ping.

## Bread and Butter Sonnet

What heaven it is to bite into fresh bread,
Inhale its yeasty odour, crush its crust,
And when thickly with butter it is spread,
To chew, to munch, to gulp with joyful lust;
But when this orgy's held in steaming tub,
With water bubbling fragrantly around,
It heightens pleasure in this simple grub -
A state of absolute Nirvana's found.
And should a blob of butter stain your skin,
The answer is at hand, it's no surprise:
There's a huge finger bowl to dip your pinkies in
While smacking lips and tasting paradise.
If you spend millions, pleasure soon would cloy,
It is small things that bring one lasting joy.

## Food, Glorious Food

*(But don't do this!)*

Life's not worth living without food,
By food I mean the golden, crispy kind,
Dripping in fat, inducing festive mood,
Good for the soul, stimulus for the mind.
Also there's cream billowing from a bun,
Jam squelching out of doughnuts - my delight,
Normandy butter glowing like the sun,
Fresh, fragrant chips are such a heartening sight.
I hate steamed fish - it's just a waste of space.
Ev'n covered with a sauce- who'd go for that?
Dip it in batter, miracles take place.
Our tastebuds ping to saturated fat.
    You ask, 'And what about your self-control?'
    No need - my STATINS zap cholesterol!

## None So Queer

Strange silent woman
stalking past
eyes sliding sideways
mouth barely twitching
in reply to greeting
crashing your door shut
against invaders.
Strong striding woman
why are your lights on
all night long?
Are you afraid
of the dark?

## Purple Sonnet

Colour of mourning and of penitence
Symbol of power and the might of kings,
Brushing the mountains with magnificence,
Softening the fall of night with purple wings.
Sugar encrusted plum, mouthwatering grape
Both bear the mark of your delightful hue,
But bursting lungs and gasping mouths agape
Show us the harsher, darker side of you
As do sore bruises, shadows under eyes
And purple blotches on a fevered skin
That troubled mothers dread when baby cries.
Yet we remember: lilac sweet as sin.
A myriad things your sumptuous shades embrace
And just like us. you often change your face.

## Sonnet Ensuite

A warm bath is a thing of pure delight ;
Womb-like, it laps us in our liquid nest,
Far from the angry shower's waspish bite,
Cuddled and coaxed to lie in utter rest.
Our hazy thoughts curl upwards with the steam,
Muscles untangle like magicians' knots;
With half closed eyes we ponder, laze and dream,
The aching soaked from our most painful spots.
No other therapy gives so much bliss,
Such peace, such calm, absence of care,
Not the most ardent lover's passionate kiss
Can with a soothing, smoothing bath compare —

There is one snag, one nagging, niggling doubt:
How long before I really MUST get out?

## Comfort

Your snoring woke me up the other night.
You grunted, gurgled, rattled round your bed
While I lay tense, waiting for morning light,
Dreading the turgid hours that lay ahead.
And then I thought of someone all alone
Whom nothing could disturb in their still room
Who had to cope with troubles on their own,
Whose house was deathly quiet as a tomb,
And so I started to enjoy the sound,
The reassuring signs that you were near,
Relaxed and closed my eyes and even found
Great comfort in the noise that I could hear.

Snore on, my love and rustle as you will —
I am so grateful that I have you still.

## Dues

For two long years I've waited for this call —
Since you went out to pay the paper bill
I've had no news of you, nothing at all
To say you were alive and kicking still.
So now you ring to say times have been bad,
You could come back if I provide the fare,
Let's start again, there's comfort to be had,
You really love me still, you know I care.
There is just one condition to fulfil
I say, one little debt you have to pay:
Please settle our two year paper bill —
Your gasp for breath shows your complete dismay.
I give a smile, replace the telephone,
What bliss to be in charge - and on my own!

## My Seven Best Things

Being grabbed by music till your heartstrings twang,
Creamy implosion of a crisp meringue,
Labyrinthine velvet of a baby's ear,
The scent of lilac like Elysian beer,
The awesome lifespan of Sequoia trees,
First summer tasting of your home-grown peas.
Lastly, (and this I'd like in my hereafter),
The raucous, bellyshaking sound of laughter.

These are the joys on which I set great store,
Tomorrow I can give you seven more.

## Bedroom Farce

The actors strut, gesticulate, orate,
Pull tragic faces, clutch despairing heads,
Doors bang like cat flaps at a furious rate,
All try to slip into adulterous beds.
The audience snickers, some guffaw aloud,
And several call to mind a stolen kiss,
Deceitful acts of which they are not proud,
Whilst others know they've done much worse than this.
The ending's happy, everything's worked out,
The lowered curtain lets the actors go,
The audience wanders home, ready no doubt
To stage their own, their very private show.
There are no new offences to commit —
You make your bed - and you must lie on it:

## Sour Sonnet on Picking Gooseberries

You're always hiding, nasty green in green
Guarded by swords which never sheathe their blades,
And half the time you scarcely can be seen,
Only with spectacles and other vision aids:
Should I be lucky and achieve my aim
Of picking enough fruit to make some pies
Then I need sugar by the bag to tame
The acid that brings tears to people's eyes.
I look at your unlovely foliage,
I see the scratches on my hand and arm
And think I must have reached a lowly stage
To grow a fruit that can do so much harm.
What makes me bother, causes me to care?
Alas, I planted you, and you are THERE!

## Woman's Best Friend

Two aged beings waddling along together,
Each trailing an ailing leg:
Her right one bulging alarmingly over crepe bandage
His left back one neatly parceled in pink plaster,
Both sniffing the scents in the summer air,
He at ground level, snuffling at canine odours
She shoving her nose into overhanging roses.
A pair of whiskery, grizzled creatures
Well past their sell-by date,
Brown coats worn into tattered patches
And each tied to the other by a long elastic lead.
But do we know who's leading whom?

## The Third Coming

*(for Benjamin, our third grandchild.*
*born May 15th, 1999*
*and with apologies to T.S. Eliot)*

A hard time we had of it
waiting for you,
but it was just the right time of year
for such an event:
the lilac billowing
and the cow parsley queening it
along the verges.
Still we waited
sleeping in snatches
listening for the call
but there was no information.
Meanwhile your mother
carried on with the struggle —
then you burst forth
not a moment too soon
perfect in every detail
puckered face frowning in concentration
tiny arms waving, busy feet kicking
in this, the first dance of your life;
and then at last we could hold you —
it was, you may say, satisfactory.

## Weekend Course on Richard Strauss

An attentive audience,
no one under fifty,
all seemingly past
the writhing stage,
watch with fascinated revulsion
the voluptuous slithering,
the sensual contortions
of poor, demented Salome
dancing in necrophiliac ecstasy
around the bleeding head
of John the Baptist.
On the over-large screen
we see her sweat glistening
as she kisses his purple lips
and we recoil —
were it not for the music,
the ravishing enrapturing music
and the sumptuous seductive singing...

Exhausted by excess
of blood and death,
still stunned by the mix
of horror and beauty,
we flee to our rooms,
try to calm down
with several cups of
camomile tea.
Thank God it's
Rosenkavalier tomorrow.

## Paradise Retold

All was peaceful and calm
in the Garden of Eden.
The bees were buzzin'
and the animals feedin'
when Eve said to Adam,
'That snake's full of jollity —
he told me those apples
are of A1 quality.
Why don' we try one
off that special tree?
It'll be full of juice
and vitamin C!'

Adam' face fell,
'you know it's verboten —
HIMSELF has said so,
it's the one he dotes on.'
But when Eve went all sulky
he gave in and picked one,
and at once HIMSELF knew
that Adam had nicked one;
so the archangel bouncers
threw them out on the spot —
All their crying and wailing
didn' help them one jot,
and outside they stood
with desolate hearts
trying to cover
their personal parts.

Now what do you think
of this bigoted tale?
It' perfectly obvious
that the author was male!
but what REALLY happened
I'll tell and I'll show:
It was Adam who started it.
Feeling macho
he bit into an apple,
ate more and still more
and when he had finished
he gave Eve the core.

So he was thrown out,
most roughly ejected
and Eve had to follow him.
sad and dejected
and she had to sew
from animal skins
those pieces of clothing
to cover HIS sins.
And when their son Cain
went round killing and maiming,
that was caused, she was told,
by bad potty training!
Don't all of you think
It's a blooming shame
that whatever happens
SHE gets the blame?

## To Each His Own

*For David*

As a small boy
he lay on the floor
thin legs outstretched
constructing the track
pushing the train with delicate hands
face frowning earnestly
in great concentration.

Now as a young man
he lies on the floor
muscular body outstretched
constructing the track
pushing the train with large gentle hands
while his two year old daughter
plays quietly beside him
face frowning earnestly
at her dolls.

## Two Year Old DIY

*For Hannah*

The two year old was taught to say,
'Happy Birthday,'
and she said it.
She was taught to say,
'Merry Christmas,'
and she said it.
She was taught to say,
'Happy New Year,'
and she got stuck.
So she said,
'Happy... happy ME!'
and that was good enough for us.

## The subject is 'Heroes'

As for me, you can keep your well-known heroes:
After all, one man's Saddam is another man's Dayan,
One man's Hitler another's Churchill
And all their actions have led to the shedding of blood.
Alexander(Great or General), Wellington, Blucher,
Even the saintly Joan, fierce Boadicea,
Olly North and Stormin' Norman
We know their deeds have caused the deaths of thousands.

No, give me the gentle ones, the
Backroom boys of fame:
Those who rescue old dears from the fire
Then disappear bashfully in a puff of smoke
Before the engines arrive;
Quiet ones who grapple scared cats from trees
Then bow out gracefully, scratched and smiling
Without giving their names;
Valiant daughters nursing obstreperous mothers —
Neither young and one entering second childhood.
Caring people washing the unsavoury
Patient people loving the unlovable
These are the unknown warriors I salute

My unflung, unsung heroes.

## The Beginning and the End

When it is time to go
the baby is decanted into the car
and she starts waving, waving
and blowing aerial kisses through the windscreen.
The last thing we see as they drive off
is a tiny, imperious hand waving,
waving for all she is worth —
she is so proud that she can do it.

When it is time to go
the old woman begs,
don't forget to come to the window
on your way out - and so we leave,
tap on the pane, and she starts waving,
waving and blowing aerial kisses through the glass.
The last thing we see as we drive off waving,
is a knobbly old hand waving for dear life
because that is all she can do .

## Talking About Refugees

*For Sarah*

Your roots are firmly set
in English soil,
your family surrounds you —
and yet your heart is large enough
to feel for people wandering,
dragging behind them weights of pain.

You tell their story to your four-year old
quietly, to make her understand
but not to fear,
your younger child held in your arms
and with a gentle hand you stroke them both,
grateful that they are near.

## The Prodigal Poet

I am the mother of many children
most of them rosy-cheeked, appealing mites,
polite in company, soft on the ear
and liked by everyone;
but just a few are squint-eyed brats,
harsh-voiced, demanding,
inclined to stamp their feet,
curse, spit in your face -
they can't be seen in public but
these are my favourite kids,
these are the ones close to my heart.

## September 11th 2001

*for Connor, when he's older*

Our four year old
rushed in
huge-eyed.
'Some planes
with people in them
have crashed into
two towers and
they're falling down!'
He then got out
his wooden bricks and
built twin towers,
surrounded them
with trees and cows and
grazing sheep and
felt he'd set
the world to rights.
I wish...

## Haiku

Smoke from our peace pipes
Recalls the bitter stench of
Smouldering battlefields

## Split Level

We are the owners of two gardens:
one, close to us is
civilised, cultivated,
respectful geraniums, dignified begonias
stand in orderly ranks,
squirrels flirt fearlessly around the lawn,
tits peck daintily on the bird table,
comforted by the nearness of the house,
while fat old ginger nods in the sun.

Then I go further down into our wood.
Already crows squawk their discordant warnings.
I hear hurried plops into our murky pond,
I stumble over mysterious holes
dug by unknown paws.
All around there is a furtive rustling,
fierce, feral smells assail me
and, as I peer through the trees,
two ears appear and a knowing rust brown face
is watching me... watching
before fading into the bushes.

I feel an intruder here.
This place is full of hidden folk
with spines and fur and wings and scaly skin,
a myriad of them and more
I shall never hear or see.
This garden does not belong to us -
it is theirs.

Time to return home
where Ginger saunters ponderously to meet me
and I give both of us the comfort
of a drink of milk.

## Soft Touch

When I was young
I loved velvet.
I palpated velvet cushions, curtains.
I stroked ribbons, collars, cuffs,
caressed ladies' skirts and blouses.
What an affectionate child,
they said,
how she loves touching!

Now that I'm old
I still love velvet:
the marvel of magnolia buds,
peach skin against my face,
cats' ears, the down on babies' cheeks
(both top and bottom)
and velvet clothes, of course,
my fingers crave the feel of it.
A weird old thing,
they say,
how she loves touching!
Yes, that's me —
a little bit touched...
wish someone would!

## In Praise of a Forties Landlady

*A good woman if ever there was one*

I sing the praises of Able
(So jokingly called, her name being Baker),
And Able she certainly was —
Able to nurture and comfort a nervous young teacher,
Able to cosset her with home-made jam,
Able to nurse her through quinsies and boyfriends,
Able to listen to her tales out of school,
Able to wait up when I came home late,
Able to rise early when I went out before dawn.
The fastest producer of chips in the Midlands,
Steel helmeted in curlers like Pallas Athene,
My washing always perfectly laundered,
Pressed with an old iron heated on gas
And beeswaxed to smooth its movements.
Coal fires she had, like gigantic conflagrations,
Huge sizzling breakfasts she served,
'To give you something to work on, dear.'
Hot chocolate at night, cool lemonade in the summer —
Four years of spoiling I had
And took it all much for granted;
And then I flew the nest to marry
And lo, Able too found an admirer
Who took her off south, to a house on a hill
From where she could inspect the fleet, the gulls,
Ensuring they were all ship-shape and Bristol fashion.

Her life went well, until one day,
On climbing home to her beloved eyrie
Her heart gave out.

Fifty years on I bless her still
And in my mind she is as ever - Able!

## Not a Pretty Sight

There you are waiting for the tram
sticky brown hair
greasing down your face
streaky anorak
not meeting
over bulbous bosom
bulging bare calves
overflowing tacky boots
smell of old chips
wafting from you
and soggy fag
curling smoke
in stubby fingers
but wait...

what's that gleaming
on your podgy pinkie?
A delicate ring
diamond tinted with
rosy stone aglow at its centre —

and I hope, yes I dare to hope that
someone loves ya, baby!

## Scene in a Bar

Her small brown hands
did almost all the talking,
birdlike they fluttered
blinking golden eyes;
they darted, landing lightly
took off again to hover
then looping, plunging —
how I would love to colour in
the patterns of their voyaging,
those swoops and swirls
those curves and curls -
a pity that she had to speak...

## Poet

A magpie
that's me!
I pick and peck
at scraps of
others' lives.
I seize on snippets
overheard on buses.
I snatch at specks
of oddities I see,
everything eerie,
anything weird —
I snitch
all things peculiar
and contradictory.
I sneak back
to my nest
there to transform them
into verses
fresh and rare —
but here's the snag:
there's nothing new
under the sun. . .

## Home Delivery

Hey, wait!
I feel a poem coming on.
Stop!
It's struggling to arrive,
Fighting to survive —
Hold it!
I need to pull,
I have to push —
Now out it comes
In a tearing rush;
But when it's born
Then I'm forlorn —
Until the next birth.
I feel relief
But there's been pain —
So who's bringing the
Champagne?

## Never too Old

The two old sisters
both nearing their end
spend their time
in acrimonious bickering; then,
when they decide
not to speak
for three or four weeks
what can one do?
One cannot tell them
that soon they'll have
no choice
whether to hear
or not to hear
each other's voice...

## Let's Not Mince Words

Dead is dead
What else can be said?

Not gone before,
Not joined the angelic host
Not passed through Peter's door
Not at one with the Holy Ghost.

Just dully dead
That's all to be said.

Not called to heavenly rest,
When life's labour is done,
Not joined the Eternal Quest
With reward well won.

Not slipped away peacefully
But dragged off unwillingly
Just deadly dead,
No more to be said
Except- silence.

## Or

Comfort me with apples
cooling green or glowing red
spurting juice when my teeth sink in.
Comfort me with apples.

Comfort me with roses
heavy lidded after rain
yellow, citrus scented or
raspberry perfumed, darkly red.
Comfort me with roses.

Comfort me with crystal
cold and finely cut
bearing fire and rainbows.
Comfort me with crystal.

Place four apples in a crystal bowl
surround with fragrant roses
and come to me... or
come empty handed and
I will be comforted.

## In the Wood

(1)

If I stand still
and close my eyes
the secret wildness
that pervades
this urban wood
might whisper to me,
I might feel its touch,
but I press on and
miss the moment.

(2)

See the stump
of the old elm
felled years ago
but look!
From its base
shoots dare to grow
braving the fungus.
Birth on the site of death...
good news for once.

## Last Letters from Berlin 1939/40

*(In homage to my grandparents who did not get away)*

Did your daughters know
how you hungered for their letters?
But you kept things bright,
how your flat had become a 'transit camp'
for relations leaving the country,
all those aunts and uncles waiting
for permits to go.
You write that Father now helps in the kitchen,
(he does his best) but you do not say
that this is because you are ill.
You still worry about others now
safely in England,
about their eyes, their chests,
their school reports
but the terrible truth was
that you knew how it would be.
Soon, you write, farewells
will have been said
and then you will be all alone.
What loneliness!
In a land of hatred you were consoled
by Beethoven and Schiller,
the best of Germany while awaiting
the booted footsteps of the worst.

Your brittle brown letters
so closely typed, so carefully worded
shiver and rustle in my hands.

When I hear Beethoven now
I bless him for the comfort he gave you
and try to think the best
of the land that bore him.

## Ice Maiden

Five hundred years I have lain in ice
left undisturbed in frozen purity
guarding the people against the anger of the gods.
My sacrifice was not in vain:
there have been no eruptions
no lava gushing, no volcanic rush,
it pleased the gods to have me there —
they feasted on my youth, on my virginity;
only the cold could penetrate my being.

And now these present men have dug me out,
have carried me through foetid air ,
have nipped at me like craven dogs,
have peered at me, through to the bone.
As though the first trial was not yet enough
I have to undergo these further trials.
At least the others gave me dignity,
prayed over me and buried me.
What will the new men do with me?
I, who was once so strong and fair,
will I become a peep show now?
What will the gods do when they see
my empty tomb?
Who will protect the people now?

## Job Dissatisfaction

*(In Kosovo and elsewhere)*

Bodies are so damned awkward to hide,
they keep popping up, letting down the side;
we could deal with them properly if we had the time,
dissolve them in acid or treat them with lime,
but we're always hurrying, never at leisure
so whatever we do with them is only half measure.
We fling them in pits, they sink out of sight,
then a boot sticks out, almost out of spite
to show us up, to bring us shame —
there's a foot left in it, but we're not to blame!
We burn them to ashes, powdery fine,
but there, in the middle; a small piece of spine!
We fling them in rivers, they balloon to the top
like a troublesome, weed ridden, unwanted crop.
When they are alive they are easy to quell
but once they are dead, they don't behave well.
The job's not complete, it could cause a reaction
and we, poor sods, get no job satisfaction!

## Preparations for an evening out, Summer 2005

His hair upstanding, gelled and hard
he gets his gear, his fags, his card.
Then he makes sure there's nothing he lacks-
oh yes, of course, his sharp-bladed axe.

## Values

The man who brings the eggs told me
that once, when he was young
he lived in Africa and owned
a cheetah.

"Soft she was
just like a fool!
I slept with her
played with her
sparred with her...
no harm to her at all."

When she was five she killed a man
whom she knocked from his bicycle because
he rang his bell- the cheetah hated noise.

"It was HIS fault
the signs were up
for all to see...
he should have looked!"

What about repercussions, compensation?

"None —
life's cheap out there
but we were told to have
my cheetah put to sleep...
and how I miss that cat!"

still mourned the man.

## Last Rights

*(In memory of Brian)*

You said,
don't make a fuss
when I am gone,
burn me
and shovel me away.
A body without life
is so much dross.
But you shall have
a slap-up funeral tea
and we shall raise a cup
in your fond memory
because
ignoring what you said
we cherish you
alive AND dead,
dear friend of ours!

## Lost

Last night I created a poem.
It arrived on the edges of sleep,
but then it took flight
like a thief in the night —
I thought it was mine to keep!

Last night I still owned a poem
full of magic and musical sound,
but it melted away
like ground-frost in May
and now it cannot be found.

Last night I was blessed with a poem
showing humour, wisdom and flair,
but it took to its heels —
now I know how it feels
when the lyrical cupboard is bare.

## Sudden death

*(Northern Ireland, 1997)*

He greeted her as he let her through
When the sniper struck out of the blue,
He'd smiled at me, she said.

And thought, as her own wound throbbed and stung,
It's not for US they have done this wrong.
He was so young, she said.

And then, as the ambulance rushed them along
She saw that his life
had nearly gone.

I wanted to hold him, she said.
And though they were each of a different belief
She could only think of his mother's grief.

God love him, she said.

## Haiku

Men and animals
Are much alike but it is
Man that is the beast

## Equal Opportunity

I watch you
an untidy woman
not yet middle-aged
sitting in the lounge
of your smart hotel
talking talking
your mobile 'phone
held to your left ear
while your right hand
is making notes
appointments dates
your cigarette smoke
curling in the ashtray
your half-finished meal
pushed aside.
You put down the 'phone
take a lung-scarring drag
on your third of a fag
reject the cup of cooling coffee
then dial and talk.
And so it goes on.
A greyness surrounds you —

So much communication
so much loneliness.

## Embryonic Snapshot

*(for Connor)*

Welcome stranger,
little being yet to be
floating at ease
in your amniotic cradle,
looking ancient and sage
with your bulging brow,
hands raised in greeting.
When you make your
strenuous descent into
the harsh outside
may the world treat you gently,
may you float through life
cushioned by love
and may all greet you
with outstretched arms of welco
Safe journey,
little being
yet to be.

## The Call

When I saw the old woman
She was shaking and trembling
Like a late brown leaf
Barely attached
To its anchorage
And the winter wind blowing.

I talked of this and that
Trying to soothe
Her painful ague,
To stop her plucking fingers
Torturing the blanket.

Suddenly she sat up,
Eyes jerking open,
And said quite clearly,
'I must go now —
I hear my name is being called.'

I took the chance to leave then
Murmuring that I would make enquiries,
But in my heart I prayed,
'Yes, I hope soon, oh very soon
Your call will come.'

## For Ella

I lost an old friend recently,
whose mind was sliding into blankness.
I regularly went to see her
although she had forgotten who I was —
and yet her smile confirmed she knew
that once she knew me.

Later her daughter came to reminisce,
to talk of happier times —
of a strong, vibrant woman,
loving her plants and her embroidery.
Then, as I waved her off
she turned and said,
'I meant to tell you,
I found two of your poems
carefully cut out
in Mother's jewellery box.'

As my eyes filled
I found no answer.
It seems worth while
to go on writing...

## Forgotten

Someone's been at
my past —
*had* and *went* and *did*
have all gone.
What have they done
with them?
The future's
uncertain too,
*shall* and *will* are
difficult —
*might* is a
mystery.

What happens
I wonder
when they cancel my
*now?*

## Contrasts

There he stands in his garden
A hunchbacked, shrunken old man,
Gaunt, gnarled and withered,
Greyfaced, colourless, stooping,
Almost invisible amongst his riotous charges;
Huge, brazen poppies send out their frantic signals,
Fat, virile lupins flaunt engorged pink heads,
Lettuce-like yellow roses drench the air
With lemony tang,
And dark, bursting paeonies release fine sprays
Of swooning odour;
And I think,
How good that it's not just the young and the fair
Who can create such an orgy
Of beauty.

## England After Iceland

*July 1992*

Oh the lovely luscious green of it,
The shining, sparkling sheen of it,
The bursting fruitful splendour
After the gaunt, cadaverous grandeur —
How good it is to be in England
Now that Summer's here.

## For a Lady Who Wanted No Fuss

*(For Nadine)*

We did
what you wanted:
a plain service,
just a few prayers,
one hymn, and then
into the flames.
But as they dug
the little hole
among the snowdrops
I thought:
all right, dear friend,
no fuss, but
you WILL arise,
pure shining white,
heralding Spring.

## Good News

Despite the bombs,
the smoke, the deaths,
the agony of every cry,
our frogs are keeping to their plans:
the pool is bubbling with their fry!

## Dumbing Down

She had once been a poet
a teacher, a left wing rebel
and now at ninety-two they gave her
a woolly toy dog.
They sat it in her window
'to make you feel less lonely
and to keep the thieves away'.
Then they kept urging her
'show them how you can bark
Grannie, go on, show them',
and she yapped away

proudly...

## Beholder

My dear old love
says I am beautiful.
I look so young,
my eyes are bright —
he's not just being dutiful,
he's got great trouble with his sight!

## Autumn

Autumn must be a cello, being so full
of mournful cadences
sun ever more diluted
greyness in light and air
even a fine day contains
a frisson of departure.
Then all at once
there's mayhem in our gardens
and Armageddon in the parks:
fires, howling shells, explosions,
the stink of cordite and of smoke
stinging our nostrils -
fun for the kids, but reminding us
(as though we need reminding)
of daily news-reports from war torn places.
By then the Christmas lights
have been strung up
and we are shoved unwillingly
into ever increasing preparations
for Winter and its forced excitements.
Instead of shopping hectically
in stale-aired stores
we should step on the lawn and study
the tissue paper frailty
of fallen leaves .....

## Haiku

After drought, soft rain
falls like a benison on
upturned faces.

## Closer by Phone

*(For Lottie)*

My aunt is twenty years older
than me, but it's getting less...
Who else can I talk to
about the old times?
Yesterday she can't remember,
tomorrow is a closed book
but ah, when she was young
and I was a child —
we talk of the country we left,
of coffee under the limes
and summer suppers on the balcony,
of Omi's fragrant chicken soup,
of walks in spicy forests,
but, she says, all the time
Death was there, outside the door.
So we must talk of brighter things,
of gardening, home helps and grandchildren
and I have to make her laugh
by recounting small domestic mishaps
like wasps' nests, leaking taps or
irregular bin collections.

When she has gone
there will be no one who has known
my early years, and part of me
will have shut down.
It's only natural, you say —
I know, but I shall grieve.

*(My aunt and I escaped from Hitler before the war)*

## Achilles

I seem to have intimations
of immortality -
other people's cancers
strokes, heart attacks
crippling arthritis
nervous diseases
mental disturbances
I grieve over,
but always I feel clad
in the armour of immunity ,
dipped in the river
of untouchability —

yet deep down
and deeper still I know that
my heel is dry.

## English Summer

Smug, we sit at home
watching the waters rise. Then —
Help! Where is the ark?

## on Appetit

ll through my life, though childless,
have loved the act of feeding:
ıts, whether mangy or embonpoint —
ɔw I've enjoyed their gutsy munching
ıd head-tilting crunching;
ɔgs, whether scrawny or grossly obese,
hat a delight to see their avid swallowing
ıd porcine wallowing.
irds, hopping nervously, pecking frenziedly,
ɔw good it is to see my crumbs swelling their gullets,
pecially geese, gabbling importantly, grabbing importunately,
hat fun to watch their quarrelsome hawking and gluttonous squawking.
s for people - there's nothing sweeter to my ears than,
Yes, I'll have a drop more of your soup,
ɔur quiche, your spinach dish."

ɔ when they come to bury me
s I've asked not to be burnt)
ere'll be an open invitation to the worms,
Yes, do come in, just help yourselves,
ɔn Appetit!"
nd then together we will feed
small piece of this famished earth.

## Boundaries

I love lilac in all its shades:
creamy white, like frothing milk,
with tickly, lemony tang,
nocturnal purple, flaunting its
heavy, headswimming odour,
but best of all lilac coloured lilac,
mother of pearl florets dangling,
breathing out beery, intoxicating fumes.

I revel in them all
plunging my face into the flowers
feeling the cool bounce of them
against my skin.

## Inhale

Oh, I would like to shower
under a waterfall of lilac
gulping its fragrance with my open mouth.
I want to wallow on a bed of lilac
crushing the blossoms with my weight,
releasing all of their secrets.
An eerie thought:
What if I were to fill my hands
with the dark lilac
squeezing until its inner juice
drips through my fingers?
Would this extract the essence or
would I breathe in the stench
of purple blood?

I leave the miracle intact
mourning the limitations of the senses.

## England - January 1991

In the bleak midwinter

On my windowsill,

A tender golden primrose

Opened its scented bill.

I touch it very gently

With careful, wondering hands,

And thank God I'm not fighting

In stinking desert sands.

I see it's fragile budding

Waiting to unfold

And think of some young people

Who will not now grow old.

Oh precious yellow flower,

You shimmer like a light —

How good to be in England

On this dark winter night.

## Brown Hands I Do Not Love

I look at them
speckled with brown
like hens' eggs used to be —
aged appendages
attached to my arms.
They are older than me
the rest of me is trim and smooth.
How do they manage to be
both fat AND wrinkled?
I will not acknowledge them.
I shall wear purple gloves
to go with Jenny Joseph's hat
and treat them like the strangers
that they are.

## Beware

Our past
pads behind us
a docile dog
coming to heel
only when called.
Don't be deceived —
one day it may pounce and
bite...

## Tortoise

She lives alone
her house a shell
around her
each musty smell
each dusty pane
anchors her to her past
forming her present.

When someone calls
her head slowly
pokes out.
she blinks, then quickly
pulls back
back into the safety
of her carapace.

O do not try
to move her into
hygienically correct
surroundings.
Out of her house
she'd shrivel and be lost
having no present
and no past and certainly
no future.

Hope that she does not
fall
nor suffer sudden
illness.
Pray that she leaves
quietly
in her sleep
without knowing...

## Thoughts of Abroad

*or Winter in Post-War Britain*

*(With abject apologies to Robert Browning)*

Oh, not to be in England
Now that winter's here,
And whoever wakes in England
Sees each morning with despair
The moisture running down the window pane,
And the damp patch sprouting on the wall again,
Whilst influenza heats each fevered brow,
In England - now!

And after this there's worse to follow,
When aching throats make it hard to swallow:
Hark how my fretful husband in his bed
Coughing and wheezing, calls me mean and cruel
To force him to inhale - I wrap the towels around his aching head

Here comes the coalman- he says he is short of fuel
Lest I should think he might be delivering
Sufficient coal to stop us folk from shivering!
And on the line the washing drips and moulders
Whilst chilblained hands massage rheumatic shoulders,
And in the frozen gloom outside the snowdrops cower -
Give ME that 'gaudy melon flower'!

## Too Much Fugits

I've been up to my eyes in mountains of photographs
having a clear-out after fifty five years,
so many birthdays, cakes, weddings, Christmasses,
holidays, outings, celebratory meals;
so many candles,cheeks puffed out for blowing,
bottles of bubbly, wine, lemonade —
seeing these loaded and groaning tables
have we really been guzzling over five decades?
And then there's the sadness of the long-gone people
staring out cheerfully in all their fine clothes,
elegant, coiffured, optimistically smiling -
nothing left now but a celluloid pose.
Even our cats are a source of nostalgia,
playful, long legged, adventurous pets.
they turn into aged, arthritic old moggies
shortly before their last trip to the vet.
Sadness too at our athletic, slimmer,
vibrant, youthful, more confident selves,
and the innocent look of the very young children
displaced by teenagers' black 'tristesse'.
Then I can see these world-weary loungers
shedding their sulks, become parents too,
gazing with pride at their beaming offspring,
tenderness obvious and solicitude.
And I think of them one day turning out photos,
marvelling like us,how they too have changed
and seeing how we, their fragile old parents
visibly shrink as we show our age.

Then I think of the many who can't view this progression,
life snatched away by some devilish State
and I realise how blessed I am and how fortunate
to be here and happy after many decades.

## Too Much

I won't have lilies
in my house again.
Recently I won a posh
floral arrangement
purple and cream
with freezias, roses,
irises and lilies.
Formal it looked
and over grand
in my small house
the lilies closed
erect like holy candles.
I marvelled and enjoyed
the mingled fragrances;
and then the lilies opened
their huge rapacious beaks
exposing orange stamen tongues
that blazoned forth
funereal odours
making my eyes water.

Not here, I thought,
I've had enough
of death,
snapped off their heads
enjoyed the gentler scents
of freezias, irises and roses,
decided there and then
I am not up to
lilies.

## Vowel Trouble

My snowdrips are dripping

My tulops need lopping

Daffidols are dipping

And narcossi are sopping.

The cyclomen are all sickening

And the pinsies are pining

Whilst my nottles are prickling

And my gropes aren't vining.

Crucoses keep creaking

Pylianthus polluted

My farns are all squeaking

And the pramroses putrid.

There's something the motter

I'm always so willing

And I work like a notter —

Could it just be my spilling?

## Writer's Dilemma

With the millions of words that have been written,

the billions of words that have been said,

how can I possibly hit on

new phrases that aren't stone dead,

metaphors, similes, adverbs

as pristine as freshly baked bread?

I give up

        tomorrow.

## After a Visit to the Specialist

So you're going to live after all —
But you know you have been touched
by the brush of those ebony wings
and though you are out in the clear
and the landscape lies sunlit before you
still your ears strain for the rush
of those dreaded, breathtaking wings.

## Fireworks

Bang
my heart
exploded
a catherine wheel
of fierce delight until it fell to earth
and in the morning light you trod on it
your heavy boot
made sure no
spark was
left.

## Relativity

Time
is a
rubber band
expands for pain
snaps back with a twang for joy and pleasure.

## Tirra Lirra

It is said your favourite photo was of you holding a dying child,
So you wanted to be Mother Teresa but with boobs and boyfriends.

You, who haunted midnight operations watching with mascara'd eyes,
you end up near midnight on a theatre table, with your chest torn open.
(They say your face was untouched - white and beautiful,
as you would have wanted it to be ).

You did have pity and healing hands —
I want to think there were hands to hug you while you were dying.

You, who used and were abused by the baying pack,
could not escape their snapping at the end.

You who sought fitness and health so frenetically
but even your well - trained heart could not withstand that dreadful imp

And the world mourned —
Would there have been so many tears and flowers
had you been dumpy, middle-aged and plain?

Rest on your floral isle our Lady of Shallot
who died together with her dubious Lancelot —
Rest quiet on your island.

## The Way Things Are

The crows

are cock-a-hoop

on our crumbs

purple-black overcoats gleaming

they strut around

Al Capones of the city's

feathered brigades.

The smaller birds

the thrushes,  tits, the robins

pick up what's left

thankful for small mercies

but they are not so plump-

forever keeping a weather eye open

for those sleek, black

menacing Mafiosi.

## Tetractys Mini-Competition

Cakes

pastries

crisp croissants

squelshy doughnuts

so good for the soul, so bad for the heart.

They've managed to steal your perfume away

exquisite rose

perfect form

but no

scent,

void

just like

the shock of

well-loved singers

unable to utter a single note.

## Streets

The news on the radio was as usual bad,

Explosions and bloodbaths on the streets of Baghdad,

But as I was walking though my peaceful streets

A woman smiled at me —

She didn't know me

But she smiled at me.

And I was struck by a jolt of joy

That she was not coming there to destroy,

That I did not have to recoil in fright

In case she was padded with gelignite.

I remembered my relatives, who in our war

Had suffered greatly and were no more,

And I thanked whatever gods there be

Who had given this tranquil moment to me —

Just friendliness and good people to meet

In our quiet, peaceful, suburban street.

## Sleepless in Wolverhampton

There are worse things
than being woken
at dawn by the
monotonous cooing
of pigeons.
I know it's better than
the cracking of bullets
the crackling of flames
the crashing of masonry
            but
this does not reconcile me
to the cacophony of pigeons
at four am, an unwelcome
Hallelujah Chorus.

## And No Birds Sing

*or One Flu Over*

Never mind    no chuckling chickens
              no gabbling geese
              no dabbling ducks
What about    no croaking crows
              no twittering tits
              no rosy robins
              no pesky pigeons
              no thrilling thrushes
              no sparring sparrows?

So            no musical mornings
              no tuneful trees?

And what about no panicking people?
I won't think about that just yet.....

## Seen At The Airport

Exhausted mother, leaning back
Eyes closing, pallid features slack,
Her four year old, lively and able
Sits herself down at the computer table,
With chubby fingers plays the keys
Moving the mouse with practised ease
Ignoring us, the world, her Mummy,
Sucking voraciously on her dummy —
So well developed all in one direction
But depending on rubber for her satisfaction,
Like modern men, with their technical arts
Still bearing inside themselves stone age hearts.

## A Birthday

*(With Apologies To Christina Rossetti)*

My heart's not like a singing bird,
I'm worried that it's beating fast,
My heart's no longer young and free,
I'm frightened that it might not last.
My heart's not fit, it lets me down,
It thuds in disconcerting ways.
The trouble is I cannot tell
Whether to start to count my days.

Bring me a pheasant in a pot,
Drench it in apricots and wine;
Serve it with chips and garden peas
Followed by Christmas pud- let's dine!
Let me forget my quaking heart,
Spoil me, caress me, ease my strain,
Make this the best day of my life
Because my birthday's here again.

## Mood Swings

Longing

for solitude

for time to hear myself

tasting the music of silence

alone.

## Yearning

for bright voices

to chirp in my dull ears

to bounce balls of words between us.

Hear me!

## Mother to Daughter

You know
this not remembering lark
is not all bad;
you forget you were happy
but you forget you were sad.
Your loss has gone missing
so has your gain,
joy has escaped
but so has the...
who are you?

## Mother's Ring

There you sit on my finger
smiling with cutting brilliance
but what makes my eyes sting
is not your icy glitter
but thinking of your previous owner:
lonely, lost in a loveless marriage
(despite diamonds, cutlery, napkins and all)
who later, being frail and of no use to the Herren Volk
was gassed and turned to ash.
None of this shows on your gleaming face-
YOU are indestructable
You cannot be burnt
YOUR value increases.
How hard it is to bear that
objects can last so much longer
than people!

So, I shall wear you, use you, care for you
but do not expect me to smile back...

## MRI Scan

My head lies clutched
by you tightly encased
and through ear plugs
I still can hear
your ceaseless hammering
while all the time you scan
the inner workings of my brain
each nerve each tissue is revealed
the hollows of my sinuses
hold no more secrets now
from your all-seeing, your magnetic eye.
And yet, despite your power
you cannot discern
the mountains, lakes and valleys
I'm imagining nor can you ever read
this verse I'm writing about you.

## Mander Centre

*Wolverhampton*

The city is heaving
everyone in a hurry
smelling of alcohol
garlic and curry
a pungent blending
of many nations
when by a stall —
sudden scent
of carnations.

## Listening

*(Written after a visit to the Ashmolean Museum)*

We were moving on
through amulets and funerary vessels
models of farmers still bringing in the corn
to keep the mighty lord content
even in this, the valley of the dead;
and onwards still, past large imposing coffins
of princes, ministers and court officials,
of Pharaoh himself, lying in dazzling gold,
when suddenly I caught a glimpse
of a small, slender cartonnage
and you reached out to me,
your song, oh Meresamun
captured me —
across nearly three thousand years
a thin wisp of a chant
wound itself round my ears
through mouldering bandages
through painted covering
gently it spun from your glass case
and I could hear you, little Meresamun,
dancer and songstress of the god Amun
in many gated Thebes.

## Last of the Mohicans

A sombre afternoon
on the last day of November
rain already splattering
thunder threatening
but just in time
the pruning has been done
There, in the gloom
on the kitchen table
three pink-petalled roses
velvety, radiant
still summer scented
breathing out hope.

## Late Rose

Today I sniffed
the last of summer.
I plunged my face
into your perfect petals
cool as a chilled child's face
inhaled the scent
of azure days
and warm voluptuous nights.

## Omi (Granny)

The child stood, ready packed

reaching up to kiss her grandmother goodbye.

(She would do this in dreams for years to come).

The old woman grimaced a smile,

touched the child's head in blessing;

then, as the steps receded

felt her life's skein unwinding —

and as she sank down, hollowed out,

knew that soon the men in boots would come

to herd her to an unspeakable end.

Anguish and terror flooded in

but there was triumph too:

The child, the child would be safe

in a kinder land...

I was that child

and I am grateful.

## Flowers of Beslan

*September 2004*

They were dressed to kill
full of joyful anticipation
boys- like little men
in long-trousered suits
girls wearing their best new frocks
all carrying flowers for teacher
huge bunches of flowers
soon to be ripped into bloody fragments.
Fresh flowers now on their muddy graves.

## Downbeat

*(For Katie)*

My old aunt said
I don't want anyone crying
at my funeral
so play some Strauss
and think of me dancing.
But when we heard The Blue Danube .
trilling around the Crem
it was the saddest sound
in the world.

## Christmas Spirit 2005

Whilst others are killing
hatred turning them wild
a Moslem mother gives
her dead son's heart
to a Jewish child.

Shalom!

## Creativity

So your old Ma's got into print!
'Jolly good, Mum', they cry in polite admiration,
eyes swivelling past to gaze at the deft gyrations
of their very own, their unique creation:
after all, how can one compare the joy
of dull, dusty words with that of a two-year old boy?
I can see their point...

## An Die Musik

*(With Schubert and Co. in mind)*

Of all the arts this is the only one
That stimulates,enraptures, gently heals.
You can enjoy it when your sight has gone,
All dances need it, waltzes, marches, reels.
The old sway gently, stretching creaking limbs,
The young must have it loud on every street,
And cracked old lips quaver out ancient hymns,
Few feet resist its life-enhancing beat.
Like all good things it can be overdone,
Polluted,stressing only raucous noise,
But hear it at its best- and like the sun
Warm on your face, it brings back natural poise.
So, when I am aware my end is near
It's Mozart's divine notes I want to hear.

## Lucy

On strong sturdy legs
and with plump imperious arms
she conducts the music
of her three year old world.

## A Cometal Tale

Hail to thee
Hale- Bopp
twinkling apparently
benignly in the velvet heavens
peacock-like flaunting
your glorious tail;
or are you perhaps
glaring at us
with your one chill eye?
Only a little nudge
and we'd be in your path—
our puny, insect lives
would finish with a bang.

But here's a thought
Oh mighty Bopp:
can you add two and two
Can you make music?
Hey, Hale-Bopp
can you smile?

## Appearances

The big man sits
On the station bench
exboxer if ever I saw one
now club bouncer I guess
mastiff faced
menacingly bald
dark jowled
sausage fingers clutching
mobile phone to
cauliflower ear.
In a loud harsh croak
he enquires
Are you feeling better, darlin'?
What does Mum say?
Mind you keep warm.
Bye now, sweetie,
Take care...
It's a bit like
sonatas tinkling
from a big bass drum.

## Pain

We are not grateful enough
when it stops —
while it is there we beg, we howl,
we promise anyone anything,
like the young queen in Rumpelstiltskin;
and as it fades, our straw of pain
is spun into the gold of ease;
we start to breathe again,
but then our thoughts begin to wander
and we grow
casual, careless, confident
forgetting that the slimy thing has only crawled
a little distance from us and lies coiled
pulsating slyly, taut, ready to strike again,
to sink its venomous fangs
into our soft, protesting tissues.

But if we were for ever grateful
we'd be for ever fearful too —
so possibly ingratitude is best?

## As Chimney-sweepers...

When you've got to go
You've got to go!
Don't ask to check the lock
Or pause to wind the clock,
Time's up!

Don't look up your account
To tot up the amount;
You can't put out the cat,
You have no time for that —

No, no,
It's time to go!
You can't look in the glass
to see if you will pass,
You'll pass alright —
Through the black gate,
Never mind your state,
Go just as you are,
With pimple and scar;
And when you've lost your grip
You'll start on your last trip,
Wild-haired,
Unprepared,
Scared,
Into the dark.

## Lament of a Poet / Housewife

When I die

I'm afraid I may only

be remembered for my

TRIFLES

**ISBN 1-905126-64-6**

Ruth Parker came to this country as a child refugee just before the Second World War, having had to leave many of her relatives behind - a fact which has clearly influenced her work; but it has also made her grateful for the happy and creative life she has been able to lead as a wife, mother, grandmother and as a writer. She taught in schools in and around Birmingham and in Wolverhampton where she has made her home for the last thirty six years.
She does not aspire to write 'great poetry' but aims to reach the core of certain events and experiences and to present them in such a way that they find an echo in her readers' imagination. She also takes great pleasure in making people laugh, which explains the wide range of subjects and styles in the collection. She hopes to go on writing till she drops.

**£6.00**

19051 26646